SIDEWAYS STORIES FROM WAYSIDE SCHOOL

by
Louis Sachar

Teacher Guide

Written by
Rachel Still

Note

The Avon paperback edition, ©1978 by Louis Sachar, was used to prepare this guide. Page references may differ in other editions.
Novel ISBN: 0-380-73148-7

Please note: Please assess the appropriateness of this book for the age level and maturity of your students prior to reading and discussing it with them.

ISBN 1-58130-865-5

Copyright infringement is a violation of Federal Law.

© 2004 by Novel Units, Inc., Bulverde, Texas. All rights reserved. No part of this publication may be reproduced, translated, stored in a retrieval system, or transmitted in any way or by any means (electronic, mechanical, photocopying, recording, or otherwise) without prior written permission from Novel Units, Inc.

Photocopying of student worksheets by a classroom teacher at a non-profit school who has purchased this publication for his/her own class is permissible. Reproduction of any part of this publication for an entire school or for a school system, by for-profit institutions and tutoring centers, or for commercial sale is strictly prohibited.

Novel Units is a registered trademark of Novel Units, Inc. Printed in the United States of America.

To order, contact your local school supply store, or—
Novel Units, Inc.
P.O. Box 97
Bulverde, TX 78163-0097

Web site: www.educyberstor.com

Lori Mammen, Editorial Director
Andrea M. Harris, Production Manager/Production Specialist
Kim Kraft, Product Development Manager/Curriculum Specialist
Suzanne K. Mammen, Curriculum Specialist
Heather Johnson, Product Development Specialist
Jill Reed, Product Development Specialist
Nancy Smith, Product Development Specialist
Pramilla Freitas, Production Specialist
Adrienne Speer, Production Specialist

Table of Contents

Skills and Strategies

Thinking
Research, compare/contrast, problem solving, creative and critical thinking, inferring, predicting, evaluating, supporting judgments

Comprehension
Main ideas and supporting details, recalling, questioning, summarizing

Vocabulary
Synonyms, antonyms, multiple-meaning words, idioms, root words, using a thesaurus/dictionary

Literary Elements
Figurative language, setting, character's traits and motivations, author's purpose, theme

Writing
Creative writing, how-to writing, newspaper journalism, poetry

Listening/Speaking
Discussion, debate

Across the Curriculum
Math—computation; Art—illustration

Genre: humorous fiction

Setting: Wayside School, which is 30 stories high and has one classroom on each story

Point of View: third person

Themes: the difference between right and wrong

Summary

Wayside School has 30 classrooms, each stacked one on top of the other; it is 30 stories high! *Sideways Stories From Wayside School* features 30 humorous episodes about Wayside School's teachers and students. Underlying every humorous and strange tale is a moral stressing the importance of good values.

About the Author

Louis Sachar studied to be a lawyer, but he did so well writing children's books that he became an author instead. He likes to write stories that are fun, but Sachar also believes in encouraging thinking about right and wrong. Sachar received a Newbery Medal for his book *Holes*. He also won the National Book Award for Young People's Literature. *Holes* is the first book to win both awards in the same year. The book has been made into a movie. Sachar wrote his first children's story as a high school assignment. "Apple Power" was about a mean teacher named Mrs. Gorf who turned students into apples. Sachar's teacher thought the story was silly and asked him to write another. Louis Sachar is married and has one daughter. The family lives in Austin, Texas.

Characters

Mrs. Gorf: the meanest teacher in the school; is turned into an apple

Mrs. Jewls: replaces Mrs. Gorf; is horribly afraid of cute children

Joe: a boy with curly hair who can't count

Sharie: a girl who always wears a red and blue overcoat and spends all of her time looking out the window or sleeping

Todd: a well-mannered boy who is constantly in trouble

Bebe: a girl who draws fast, but not well

Calvin: a boy who teams up with Bebe to create quick art; he is also asked to deliver a note to a teacher who does not exist at Wayside School

Myron: a boy who is chosen class president and becomes a hero by saving a dog

Maurecia: a girl who likes nothing, but whom everyone likes

Paul: a boy who sits behind Leslie and pulls her pigtails

Dana: a girl who is encouraged to learn math by counting her mosquito bites

Jason: a boy with a big mouth who is stuck to his seat with chewing gum

Rondi: a girl who is missing her two front teeth and is frustrated by jokes that she does not understand

Sammy: a stinky student who turns out to be a dead rat

Deedee: a girl who finds out that getting a high-bouncing ball during recess is not an easy task

D.J.: a boy with a secret smile that causes curiosity among Mrs. Jewls' students

John: a boy who can only read words that are written upside down

Leslie: a girl with pigtails who doesn't know what to do with her toes

Miss Zarves: a teacher who does not exist at Wayside School

Kathy: a girl who assumes no one will ever like her and is proven right

Ron: a boy who insists on playing kickball even though he is a terrible player

The Three Erics: three boys named Eric who are confused with one another, although all three boys are very different; Eric Bacon (Fatso) is not fat, Eric Ovens (Crabapple) is not mean, and Eric Fry (Butterfingers) is not clumsy

Allison: pretty girl with a sky-blue windbreaker; learns an important secret about teachers

Dameon: a boy who misses a class movie because he is running up and down the stairs from his classroom to the playground

Jenny: a girl who arrives at school on Saturday and is questioned by mysterious men

Terrence: a boy who kicks all the playground balls over the fence

Joy: a girl who steals Dameon's lunch and places the various wrappers on other students' desks

Nancy: a boy who does not like his name

Stephen: a boy who scares away the ghost of Mrs. Gorf

Louis: the yard teacher at Wayside School; tells the children a story about a one-story school

Initiating Activities

1. Preview the Book: Direct students to look at the book title and cover for *Sideways Stories From Wayside School*. Ask: What do you think this story will be about? Do you think chapters in the book will be funny or serious? Have you read any other books by Louis Sachar? Have students make some predictions and list their responses.

2. Predict: Have a student read the back cover aloud. Relate the information given on the front cover to what the student has read. As a class, predict what the story will be about.

3. Make Predictions: Have students read the chapter titles and examine the chapter illustrations. Ask students to make predictions about what they are going to read in each chapter. Students should record their predictions on pages 7–8 of this guide and review them after reading the book.

4. Explore a Humorous Situation: Ask students to imagine themselves as students at Wayside School. Read this scenario aloud to the class: You are stuck to your seat by a wad of chewing gum. How do the teacher and students free you?

5. Anticipation Questions: Have students fill out the Anticipation Guide on page 6 of this guide. Try to elicit the reasoning students have for their choices.

6. Attribute Web: Create an attribute web (page 9 of this guide) with students for each of the following ideas: things that are silly, things that are strange, friendship.

7. Writing: Have students write summaries that contain the main ideas of a reading section and the most significant details. Students can also write responses to the novel as they read. Students should support their judgments through references to both the text and prior knowledge. Finally, students can write stories based on the novel. They should use concrete sensory details to relate a wacky event or experience.

8. Brainstorming: Ask students to list synonyms for the words "strange" and "silly."

Vocabulary Activities

1. Thesaurus: Students should use a thesaurus to determine ten related words and concepts.

2. Multiple-meaning words: Students should locate five multiple-meaning words from the novel and interpret their meaning. Some examples are: "hood" (p. 16) and "star" (p. 22).

3. Root words: Students should use their knowledge of root words like "amaze" in the word "amazement" (p. 19), and "value" in the word "valuable" (p. 22), to determine the meaning of five unknown words in the novel.

4. Synonyms/Antonyms: Students should apply their knowledge to determine the meaning of five words and two phrases from the novel.

5. Dictionary: Students should use a dictionary to learn the meanings and other features of ten unknown words. Students can arrange a group of vocabulary words in alphabetical order to create a mini-dictionary.

6. Summaries: Students should select three to five vocabulary words from each group of chapters to write summaries that contain the main ideas of the reading selection and the most significant details.

7. Idioms: Students should locate and explain idioms used in the novel; for example, "Todd had three strikes against him" (p. 22).

8. Figurative Language: Students should locate and explain figurative language used in the novel; for example, "When he got an idea, his eyes lit up" (p. 19).

Anticipation Guide

Directions: Read each of the following statements. Write a T for true or an F for false. Discuss your responses with a partner. After you have completed the novel, discuss the statements again.

1 ———— 2 ———— 3 ———— 4 ———— 5 ———— 6
strongly agree   strongly disagree

	Before	After
1. There is only one way to solve a problem.	_____	_____
2. Without rules, children will not behave.	_____	_____
3. All teachers are kind.	_____	_____
4. Children can be heroes.	_____	_____
5. The best kind of art takes time to create.	_____	_____
6. If something stinks, it is probably a rat.	_____	_____
7. Children who are missing their front teeth have the most beautiful smiles.	_____	_____
8. Behaving can get you into trouble.	_____	_____
9. You can learn math by counting mosquito bites.	_____	_____
10. Some people learn best when they stare out of a window.	_____	_____

Using Predictions

We all make predictions as we read—little guesses about what will happen next, how a conflict will be resolved, which details will be important to the plot, which details will help fill in our sense of a character. Students should be encouraged to predict, to make sensible guesses as they read the novel.

As students work on their predictions, these discussion questions can be used to guide them: What are some of the ways to predict? What is the process of a sophisticated reader's thinking and predicting? What clues does an author give to help us make predictions? Why are some predictions more likely to be accurate than others?

Create a chart for recording predictions. This could either be an individual or class activity. As each subsequent chapter is discussed, students can review and correct their previous predictions about plot and characters as necessary.

Use the facts and ideas the author gives.

Use your own prior knowledge.

Apply any new information (i.e., from class discussion) that may cause you to change your mind.

Predictions
_____
_____
_____
_____

Prediction Chart

What characters have we met so far?	What is the conflict in the story?	What are your predictions?	Why did you make these predictions?

Attribute Web

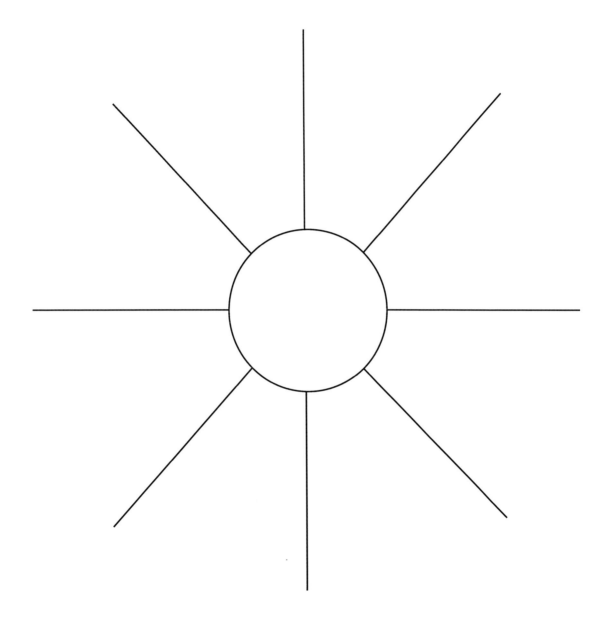

Venn Diagram

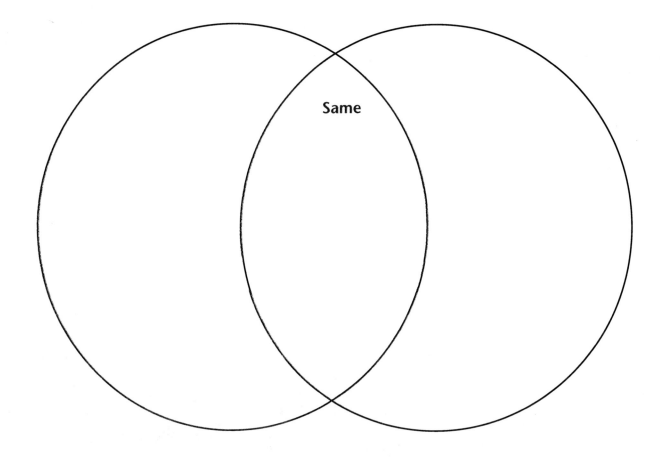

Same

Introduction & Chapters 1–5, pp. 1–22

The children on the thirtieth floor of Wayside School are turned into apples by their wicked teacher, Mrs. Gorf. Her curse is reversed when Mrs. Gorf is herself turned into an apple and then accidentally eaten. Mrs. Jewls replaces Mrs. Gorf and establishes rules and routine. Joe is a student who counts the wrong way but is able to get the right answer. Sharie often falls asleep in class. While asleep, she falls out the window, and Louis catches her just before she hits the ground. Todd gets into trouble every day despite being the quietest and most hard-working student in class.

Vocabulary
accidentally (1)
investigate (5)
ridiculous (8)
confused (17)

Discussion Questions

1. How do the children at Wayside School feel about their school? (*They enjoy having a sideways school and an extra-large playgound. p. 1*)

2. Why does Louis, the yard teacher, think that Mrs. Gorf must be the best teacher in the world? (*He sees 12 apples on her desk and thinks the students have brought them to her to express their appreciation or affection for her. p. 5*)

3. Why are the children afraid of Mrs. Jewls? (*She is nice, and they have never had a nice teacher. p. 7*)

4. What does Mrs. Jewls expect of the children that Mrs. Gorf did not? (*Mrs. Jewls expects the children to follow rules and to learn. p. 10*)

5. What is special about Joe? (*He counts the wrong way but is able to get the right answer. pp. 11–12*)

6. According to Mrs. Jewls, why is school important? (*School speeds up the learning process for children. p. 15*)

7. Why does Mrs. Jewls allow Sharie to nap and to stare out the window? (*Mrs. Jewls recognizes that people learn in different ways. p. 16*)

8. Why do the children clap as Todd leaves the classroom? (*He heroically thwarts two robbers by encouraging them to learn instead of steal. p. 22*)

Supplementary Activities

1. Research: Explain how the story of Mrs. Gorf is like a fairy tale. List any fairy tale characters that Mrs. Gorf resembles.

2. Critical Thinking: Why does Mrs. Jewls establish rules for the children? Why is it significant that they are "monkeys" before the rules are established? List five important classroom rules.

3. Writing: Write an essay explaining why counting the hairs on one's head is a difficult task.

4. Critical Thinking: Joe is able to get correct answers even though he does not count in the conventional way. Brainstorm unique solutions using new ways of thinking. Using models of learning styles/divergent ways of thinking, assess your own learning style.

5. Math: Read the description of Sharie's overcoat on page 16 of the novel. Write a similar description of any object using math to describe it.

6. Problem Solving: Think about how Joy is constantly frustrating Todd in Chapter 5. Make a chart listing ways to handle problems with your peers. In the left column, write a problem you might have with a peer. In the right column, list constructive ways in which you could handle the problem.

Chapters 6–11, pp. 23–46

Calvin helps Bebe create art. Although they cooperate to get a lot done, the art is rushed and is of poor quality. Calvin is asked to deliver a note to a teacher who does not exist at Wayside School. He is ironically praised for his failed efforts. Myron is chosen class president, but finds his duties of turning the classroom lights on and off less than heroic. Mrs. Jewls helps Maurecia make friends by creating "student-flavored" ice cream. Paul is sent home from school early for pulling Leslie's pigtails. Mrs. Jewls helps Dana learn math by encouraging Dana to count her mosquito bites.

Vocabulary

masterpiece (24)
teamwork (24)
responsible (30)
unconscious (33)
heartbroken (36)
urge (39)
concentrate (44)

Discussion Questions

1. What is remarkable about the teamwork between Calvin and Bebe? (*Answers will vary. pp. 23–26*)

2. How does Bebe change as an artist? (*Bebe goes from being a fast draw to taking more time with her pictures. p. 26*)

3. Explain the last line of Chapter 7 when Calvin states that delivering the note was "nothing." (*Calvin is being ironic by saying that his nonsensical task was "nothing." p. 30*)

4. Is saving a dog more important than turning lights on and off? Why or why not? (*Answers will vary.*)

5. How does Maurecia change after tasting different flavors of ice cream? (*Maurecia likes everyone instead of no one. p. 37*)

6. Why does Leslie yell out a third time? (*Answers will vary. p. 42*)

7. In Chapter 11, how does Mrs. Jewls get the children to stop complaining and concentrate on the lesson? (*Mrs. Jewls uses the counting of Dana's mosquito bites to teach math. pp. 43–46*)

Supplementary Activities

1. Problem Solving: Write an essay describing types of school activities that encourage cooperation and teamwork.

2. Creative Thinking: Name things that you consider to be temptations. List some creative ways to resist temptations.

3. Math: Write creative math problems based on real situations.

4. Creative Thinking: Design a "fun" lesson that engages students in learning a particular concept.

5. Brainstorm: List the responsibilities of a class president. Use the list to compose a class poem, perhaps using "turning the lights on and off" as a repeated line.

Chapters 12–16, pp. 47–66

Jason is stuck to his chair with bubble gum, and the students must figure out how to free him. Rondi is frustrated by jokes that she does not understand. Sammy turns out to be a rat. Deedee finds that getting a high-bouncing ball during recess is not an easy task. D.J.'s secret smile causes curiosity among Mrs. Jewls' students.

Vocabulary
specialty (49)
disturb (53)
mousey (59)
pushover (64)

Discussion Questions

1. Why do Rondi and Allison tickle Jason? (*Their teacher leaves the room, and the two girls are tempted by the opportunity. p. 49*)

2. Why does Rondi bite Louis? (*Rondi is frustrated by the jokes made at her expense. p. 54*)

3. Why don't the students like Sammy? (*He stinks, he is mean to them, and he has a horrible voice. pp. 55–58*)

4. How does Deedee solve her playgound problem? (*Deedee goes to recess early by pretending to be a dead rat that is thrown out of class by Mrs. Jewls. pp. 61–62*)

5. Why is everyone so curious about the reason for D.J.'s smile? (*Answers will vary. pp. 64–66*)

Supplementary Activities

1. Creative Writing: Write jokes using characters from the book and perform them for the class.

2. Critical Thinking: Think of a time you felt frustrated, others laughed at you, or you were embarrassed. Write about the event in a journal.

3. Creative Writing: Write about another creative way that Deedee could get to recess early.

4. Creative Writing: Write about why you think D.J. is so happy.

Chapters 17–21, pp. 67–81

John can only read words that are written upside down. Leslie considers selling her toes to Louis. There is not a story for Chapter 19 because there is not a nineteenth floor or a teacher named Miss Zarves. Kathy thinks the other children are ugly and stupid, and the only student Kathy likes turns out to be a dead rat named Sammy. Ron is terrible at playing kickball but wants to play it every day. Louis, the yard teacher, allows Ron to play kickball to teach the children to share and to include others in their games.

Vocabulary
balance (68)
furious (73)
insisted (76)
inning (80)

Discussion Questions

1. What is Mrs. Jewls' solution to John's problem? (*Mrs. Jewls suggests that he learns to stand on his head to read. p. 68*)

2. Why does Louis offer Leslie more for her hair than for her toes? (*Answers will vary. p. 73*)

3. Why is the absence of a story for Chapter 19 funny? (*Answers will vary. p. 74*)

4. Why is it ironic that Kathy only likes Sammy? (*Sammy is an obnoxious dead rat that no one likes, and Kathy is herself somewhat obnoxious. p. 75*)

5. What would make a reader dislike Kathy? (*Kathy judges others without knowing them and situations without giving them a chance to work. p. 75*)

6. Even though his team never wins, why does Ron want to play kickball? (*Answers will vary. pp. 78–81*)

Supplementary Activities

1. Research: Research dyslexia. How does this condition relate to John?

2. Creative Writing: Write a story about the nineteenth floor and Miss Zarves.

3. Art: Create an illustration for a chapter in this section.

4. Journalism: Rewrite one chapter as a newspaper article for an imaginary Wayside School Newspaper.

Chapters 22–26, pp. 82–102

There are three boys named Eric in Mrs. Jewls' class. The students confuse them with each other, although the three boys are very different. Allison learns that children are really smarter than their teachers. Dameon misses a class movie because he is running up and down the stairs from his classroom to the playground. No one is at school when Jenny arrives because it is Saturday. Terrence kicks all the playground balls over the fence, so Louis kicks Terrence over the fence.

Vocabulary
fly (83)
tangerine (86)
hazel (89)
puzzled (95)
underhand (99)

Discussion Questions

1. How are the nicknames of the three Erics wrong for each boy? (*Eric Bacon [Fatso] is not fat, Eric Ovens [Crabapple] is not mean, and Eric Fry [Butterfingers] is not clumsy. pp. 82–84*)

2. Why is Allison eager to help her teachers? (*They always help her. pp. 86–88*)

3. How can Dameon solve his problem instead of wasting time? (*Answers will vary. pp. 89–92*)

4. Why is Jenny questioned when she arrives at school late? (*It is Saturday. pp. 94–97*)

5. How does the author build suspense in Chapter 25? (*Jenny grows increasingly nervous when questioned by strangers, and the author does not reveal until the last sentence that it is Saturday. pp. 93–97*)

6. Why is Terrence a bad sport? (*He kicks the balls over the fence. pp. 98–102*)

7. Is Terrence's consequence fair in Chapter 26? Why or why not? (*Answers will vary. p. 102*)

Supplementary Activities

1. Critical Thinking: Do you agree or disagree with the statement that children are smarter than their teachers? Write an essay that provides examples to support your opinion.

2. Math: Calculate the amount of time it takes to ascend a flight of stairs. How long would it take to go up 30 flights of stairs?

3. Creative Writing: Rewrite Chapter 25 as a poem.

4. Creative Writing: Write a paragraph in which you relate an experience by building suspense.

5. How-to Writing: Read the description of the game "spud" on page 99 of the novel. Write a brief description of a game using specific details.

Chapters 27–30, pp. 103–118

Joy steals Jason's lunch and places the various wrappers on other students' desks. Nancy is a boy who does not like his name. The students and Mrs. Jewls decide to trade names. The ghost of Mrs. Gorf visits Mrs. Jewls' classroom. Stephen hugs the ghost of Mrs. Gorf and makes her disappear. Louis tells a story to the children in Mrs. Jewls' class. They don't like the story because they can't imagine a school so different from their own.

Vocabulary
evidence (105)
filching (106)
ashamed (107)
leotards (111)
blizzard (115)

Discussion Questions

1. Why does Joy take credit for being a good detective? (*Answers will vary. pp. 104–105*)

2. Why do certain foods taste like Miss Mush's porridge to Joy? (*Joy cannot forget that she stole Jason's lunch, and so the foods she stole now taste like porridge to her. p. 106*)

3. Why does Nancy become outgoing after trading names with Mac? (*Nancy was only shy because he was embarrassed about having a girl's name; now he has a boy's name, Mac. p. 109*)

4. Why does the ghost of Mrs. Gorf disappear when Stephen hugs her? (*Answers will vary. p. 114*)

5. Whom do you think the character Louis is based on? (*He is based on Louis Sachar, the author of the book.*)

6. Why does Dameon think that the school described in Louis' story is horrible? (*Dameon thinks the school is horrible because the children do not behave like the children at Wayside. p. 118*)

Supplementary Activities

1. Writing: Write an essay explaining your opinion of Joy's behavior in Chapter 27. Should Joy have gotten away with these deeds? Why or why not?

2. Research: Research the origin and meaning of your name. Would you change your name if you could? What would your new name be?

3. Creative Writing: Write a story about your classroom on the Friday before Halloween.

4. Critical Thinking: Pretend you are a student at Wayside. In an essay, explain how you feel about your school. Is it fun or scary? Give reasons to support your opinion.

5. Critical Thinking: Compare/contrast two characters from the novel using the Venn Diagram on page 10 of this guide.

6. Writing: Write a summary of the novel.

Post-reading Discussion Questions

1. Do the consequences for wrongdoings in the novel fit the characters' "crimes"? Why or why not?

2. What is your opinion of Wayside School? Cite examples to support your opinion.

3. Would you like having Mrs. Jewls as a teacher? Why or why not?

4. Compare the villain Mrs. Gorf to others you have read about.

5. Do the children change throughout the novel? Cite examples to support your answer.

6. Cite examples of heroism in the novel.

7. What makes the children at Wayside School such an unusual group?

8. Why are some of the children scared by Louis' story in Chapter 30?

9. Why is the novel especially fun for children to read?

10. Cite examples of humor in the novel.

Post-reading Extension Activities

1. Mrs. Jewls is a wacky teacher. Write about a special teacher that you have had.

2. In small groups, discuss what makes someone a hero. Is Myron a hero? Cite specific examples to support your opinion. Share your ideas with the class.

3. Using the Venn Diagram on page 10 of this guide, compare/contrast Wayside School with your school.

4. Write a story about how another rat sneaks into Mrs. Jewls' classroom.

5. Write a poem about the wacky happenings at Wayside School.

6. Perform some sideways stories from Wayside School as reader's theater. Check online resources for scripts. One cite is: Aaron Shepard's RT Page at www.aaronshep.com/rt. (Web site active at time of publication.)

7. Design a book cover for the novel. Include an illustration and book summary.

Assessment for *Sideways Stories From Wayside School*

Assessment is an ongoing process. The following eight items can be completed during the novel study. Once finished, the student and teacher will check the work. Points may be added to indicate the level of understanding.

Name _____ Date _____

Student   **Teacher**

_____   _____   1. Keep a list of words that you do not recognize, along with the page number, in a reading journal.

_____   _____   2. Keep a character chart of those you meet in the book. Include name, description, and an original illustration.

_____   _____   3. Who is Mrs. Gorf? Create a collage of ideas and images significant to her.

_____   _____   4. Write a new chapter for this novel.

_____   _____   5. Write a newspaper article about one of the wacky events in the novel.

_____   _____   6. Rewrite a chapter as a scene for a play.

_____   _____   7. In a paragraph, present the pros and cons of attending Wayside School.

_____   _____   8. As you read the novel, keep a list of wrongdoings and the consequences that characters experience for each wrong action.

Effects of Reading Writing Assessment

A. Prewriting: When reading, each part of a book may affect you in a different way. Think about how parts of the novel affected you in different ways. Did some parts make you laugh? cry? want to do something to help someone? Below, list one part of the book that touched each of the following parts of the body: your head (made you think), your heart (made you feel), your funny bone (made you laugh), or your feet (spurred you to action).

Your head	Your heart

Your funny bone	Your feet

B. Open-Ended Writing Prompt: Write a paragraph about how reading the book, *Sideways Stories From Wayside School* affected different parts of you. Include specific examples from the book in your paragraph.

Linking Novel Units® Lessons to National and State Reading Assessments

During the past several years, an increasing number of students have faced some form of state-mandated competency testing in reading. Many states now administer state-developed assessments to measure the skills and knowledge emphasized in their particular reading curriculum. The Discussion Questions and Post-reading Questions in this Novel Units® Teacher Guide make excellent open-ended comprehension questions. Teachers may also use scoring rubrics provided for their own state's competency test. *Please note*: The Novel Units® Student Packet contains an optional open-ended question in a format similar to many national and state reading assessments.

Scoring Rubric for Open-Ended Items

3-Exemplary	Thorough, complete ideas/information Clear organization throughout Logical reasoning/conclusions Thorough understanding of reading task Accurate, complete response
2-Sufficient	Many relevant ideas/pieces of information Clear organization throughout most of response Minor problems in logical reasoning/conclusions General understanding of reading task Generally accurate and complete response
1-Partially Sufficient	Minimally relevant ideas/information Obvious gaps in organization Obvious problems in logical reasoning/conclusions Minimal understanding of reading task Inaccuracies/incomplete response
0-Insufficient	Irrelevant ideas/information No coherent organization Major problems in logical reasoning/conclusions Little or no understanding of reading task Generally inaccurate/incomplete response